HiSTORY ROC
Women in Law

A century
of women's
legal history,
illustrated
by children!

Published by Guy Fox History Project Limited
Illustrated by Students at Snowsfields Primary School, London

History Rocks: Women in Law

Guy Fox History Project Limited

FIRST EDITION

Copyright © 2019 Guy Fox History Project Limited and Guy Fox Limited
www.guyfox.org.uk

ISBN 978-1-904711-28-5

This book was illustrated with assistance from students at Snowsfields Primary School whose drawings are used with their kind permission.

With thanks to Dr Mari Takayanagi, whose expertise and enthusiasm were an invaluable source of information and inspiration during the project.

Blackstone
CHAMBERS

Funded by Blackstone Chambers

Supported by volunteers from Blackstone Chambers
Printed and bound in Great Britain

TABLE OF CONTENTS

About the Project

'History Rocks: Women in Law' marks the 100th anniversary of the Sex Disqualification (Removal) Act, which allowed women to become barristers and solicitors. With the support of barristers and staff from Blackstone Chambers, the Guy Fox team worked with children from Snowsfields Primary School, London. They explored a century of women in law and created the illustrations for this book. We also met Baroness Hale, the first female President of the UK Supreme Court, and we learned how she has made history. The project was funded by Blackstone Chambers and supported by their lovely volunteers.

Drawing pictures for this book

Visiting the Supreme Court

Meeting the President of the Supreme Court, Baroness Hale

Re-enacting the passage of the
Sex Disqualification (Removal) Act

Trying on a real barrister's wig

Volunteers from Blackstone Chambers

Learning about our legal system with real
barristers from Blackstone Chambers

Re-enacting the passage of the
Sex Disqualification (Removal) Act

Introduction

On 23rd December 1919, when the Sex Disqualification (Removal) Act became a law, women were no longer prevented from entering professions.

In other words, women could become barristers and solicitors. Yippee! Even better, the law allowed women to serve on juries, become justices of the peace and work in other professions such as vet and accountant.

The law didn't do EVERYTHING that women had hoped for – women still couldn't become diplomats, for example – but it was a big step.

These days, we take it for granted that ANYBODY can do almost ANY job, but that wasn't always the case. A century ago, there were <u>lots</u> of things that women were <u>not</u> allowed to do. Being a lawyer was just one of them!

Not only was that unfair to women, it was unfair to ALL of us. After all, our society was missing out on the energy, perspective and intelligence that women could offer.

This book will tell you about life 100 years ago, explain how Parliament passed that law in 1919 and introduce you to a collection of inspiring women who have made legal history.

But this book is more than a history lesson; it's a celebration of our ongoing journey towards a fair and inclusive society – and how we can all support it as we move forward.

Happy reading!

Guy Fox

LIFE IN 1919

What was life like? Well, that depended entirely on whether you were born rich or poor, male or female.

If you were <u>RICH</u>, you'd probably live in a big house in the countryside. You'd get lots of fresh air while taking walks, going hunting or playing cricket. You'd probably have servants to do all the housework — like cooking, cleaning and looking after the children.

For your education, you might be taught by a private tutor or go to boarding school, and you'd learn maths and Latin and Greek. But you'd only learn these things if you were a boy.

If you were a girl, you'd learn the skills you'd need to attract a rich husband — reading, writing, and maybe some history or how to play the piano.

You'd probably get a
huge breakfast, then a
massive lunch with six or seven
dishes. Of course, you wouldn't
want to miss out on afternoon tea with
all those cakes and sweets and sandwiches.
Nom nom nom! And that wasn't all! You'd also eat
a huge dinner, served by your servants. Burp!

If you got sick, you could call a doctor, who'd come to your
house. Of course, you'd have to pay him; but of course, you'd be
able to — because you'd be RICH!

in all, if you were rich — and a rich man — life in 1919 was wonderful!

On the other hand, if you were <u>POOR</u>, you'd probably live in a small, dirty, crowded, rat-infested place. You'd probably be hungry a lot of the time, and when you did get food, it wasn't very nutritious. If you got sick, there was no doctor – and no National Health Service – so even a minor illness might kill you! Eek!

If your family didn't need you to work, you might go to school. If you were a boy, you'd learn maths and reading; if you were a girl, you'd learn cooking and sewing. And watch out! Teachers used the cane for discipline! All in all, if you were poor, life in 1919 was difficult.

LIFE FOR WOMEN IN 1919

If you're thinking that life in 1919 did NOT seem fair, we agree with you! For women – rich, poor or somewhere in the middle – things were even worse.

If you were a woman in 1919, there were lots of things that you weren't allowed to do. When it came to work, you didn't have many options. Certain jobs were considered "women's work" – like working in a laundry, doing sewing and mending, being a clerk in an office, or serving customers in a shop. But it was unlikely that you'd get to be the boss! And in some professions – such as teaching – you had to quit your job if you got married.

If you had other interests – for example science or law – you weren't allowed to pursue them. And you certainly weren't allowed to do them as your job!

Imagine all the ways that women could contribute to society – if only they had a voice AND a choice. The good news is, attitudes (and laws) had started to change.

Women should be allowed to:

Attend any university (including Cambridge and Oxford) and receive a degree.

Vote in a General Election (regardless of our age and whether or not we own property).

Work as barristers, solicitors, accountants or diplomats (and LOTS of other jobs!).

Work at our professions after getting married.

Be members of a professional society, like the Royal Society or the Royal Institution.

Inherit property like men do.

Serve on a jury.

Open a bank account and apply for a loan in our own name.

Receive equal pay for equal work.

Life is frustrating.

WOMEN NEEDED A VOICE

In February 1918, following a long campaign, Parliament finally passed the Representation of the People Act. This law gave more than 8 million women the right to vote in a General Election. Not long afterwards, the Parliament (Qualification of Women) Act allowed women to stand for election to Parliament. It would be another 10 years before all women would get the right to vote (thanks to the Representation of the People (Equal Franchise) Act of 1928) but it was a good start.

WOMEN NEEDED A CHOICE

Gwyneth Bebb could have contributed so much to our society, if only she'd been allowed her choice of career. She wanted to be a solicitor, so she studied Law at Oxford University and finished in 1911. If she'd been a man, she would've been awarded a degree, taken the law exams and started training.

Unfortunately, at that time, Oxford did not give degrees to women. That didn't stop Gwyneth. She tried to take the law exams, but the Law Society wouldn't let her — because she was a woman. How frustrating! Gwyneth had done all the work and had proven that she was smart enough to become a solicitor. And she wasn't alone: Nancy Nettlefold, Maud Ingram and Karin Costelloe had also been rejected.

Did You Know...?

The Parliament (Qualification of Women) Act, which gave women over 21 the right to stand for election to the House of Commons, is only twenty-seven words long! It is the shortest law in the UK.

The Law Society claimed that, according to the Solicitors Act of 1843, only men could be solicitors. The law used the word 'person' and the Law Society believed that 'person' meant 'man'.

So in 1913, Gwyneth and the other women took the Law Society to court. Their barrister, Stanley Buckmaster, asked the judges to decide that 'person' also included 'woman'. The case was dismissed, but Gwyneth did not give up. She asked Robert Cecil to be her barrister in the Court of Appeal.

The judges decided that a woman could NOT be a solicitor or barrister – simply because it had never happened before! The judges said, until there was a law that plainly said, "WOMEN CAN BE BARRISTERS AND SOLICITORS", women could not be barristers or solicitors. In our legal system, after all, a judge's job is to interpret existing laws, rather than make new ones.

If women were ever going to become barristers and solicitors, Parliament would need to make a new law!

Guy Fox presents...
Women in Law

If all we needed was a new law, then that's what Parliament did, right?!
Surely they just passed a law that allowed women to become barristers and
solicitors. Easy peasy! Well, let's not get ahead of ourselves.

We need to bear in mind a few things:

1 Law making is a process.
To become a law, a Bill needs to be introduced, debated, voted on, and
amended — and it needs to pass through both the House of Lords and the
House of Commons. This process can take a lot of time (and patience)!

2 Everyone in Parliament was a man.
In early 1919, the Houses of Parliament looked like this:

House of
Lords

House of
Commons

Can't remember how
Parliament makes laws?
Take a peek at Page 40.

Timeline

Learn more about
me (and other
History Makers)
starting on Page 22!

1854
Barbara Leigh Smith Bodichon publishes her booklet.

③ The country was recovering from the First World War.
The First World War had ended in 1918, leaving Europe in tatters. Our country was returning to normal — and trying to figure out what 'normal' was! Earlier in the year, Parliament had passed the Representation of the People Act, which allowed some women to vote. And in December, women had voted for the first time in a General Election! Some Lords and MPs felt that they'd done enough for women for the time being. They wanted Parliament to focus on laws to help the country recover.

④ The government gets to set the agenda for laws.
The current government was a coalition, with <u>Conservative</u> and <u>Liberal</u> MPs. David Lloyd George was the prime minister. These men had their own ideas about which laws to pass. It was unlikely that any other Bill — especially one proposed by the rival <u>Labour</u> Party — would get the government's support.

In the face of these challenges, the fact remained: if women were going to be allowed to be barristers and solicitors, Parliament needed to pass a new law. Fortunately, there were supportive men inside who were willing to try.

BARRISTERS & SOLICITORS (QUALIFICATION OF WOMEN) BILL

The first man to try was Lord Buckmaster*. He'd previously introduced Bills to allow women to become solicitors, but they'd failed due to uncertainty during the war. This Bill, the Barristers & Solicitors (Qualification of Women) Bill, would've done exactly what its title said: to allow women to become barristers and solicitors. But by

Barristers & Solicitors (Qualification of Women) Bill

Lord Buckmaster
*If 'Buckmaster' rings a bell, it's because he was Gwyneth Bebb's barrister!

1885
Helen Taylor <u>tries</u> to stand for Parliament.

1888
Eliza Orme is granted a Law degree.

the time it passed through the House of Lords, someone in the House of Commons had introduced a different Bill!

WOMEN'S EMANCIPATION BILL

Benjamin Spoor, a Labour MP, introduced a Private Member's Bill called the Women's Emancipation Bill. 'Emancipation' means 'freedom', and if this Bill had become a law, women would have gained a lot of it:

1) To be allowed to work at professions, including government jobs;
2) To be allowed to vote if they were over the age of 21 (same as men);
3) To sit and vote in the House of Lords.

The government was worried. If a Labour MP passed a law that allowed more women to vote – which would obviously make women happy – the Labour Party might win the next election! And that would mean Mr Lloyd George would be out of a job. Hmmm. Christopher Addison, a government minister, started grumbling that the Bill was badly written. But he didn't offer any help to rewrite it!

> A *Private Member's Bill* is a special Bill, introduced by an MP or a Lord, instead of the government.

As more and more MPs supported the Bill, the government objected more and more. (Surprise, surprise!)

The government decided to discuss the Bill with the men who worked in the civil service. Civil servants thought women shouldn't work after getting married, shouldn't take the same civil service exams as men and shouldn't work overseas. Despite all their objections and the government's protests, the Bill passed through the House of Commons. It was sent over to the House of Lords.

Benjamin Spoor

1913
Gwyneth Bebb <u>tries</u> to become a lawyer.

Representation of the People Act
February 1918

6th February 1918
Representation of the People Act

The government wants its OWN Bill!

SEX DISQUALIFICATION (REMOVAL) BILL

That's when the government introduced its own Bill! This one, the Sex Disqualification (Removal) Bill had 2 clauses:

David Lloyd George

1) To allow women to work in public jobs and serve on juries, <u>except</u> A) the civil service could make its own rules for women; and B) judges could ban women from juries if they thought the case wasn't suitable;

2) To allow women to sit and vote in the House of Lords.

This Bill was intended to kill off the Women's Emancipation Bill once and for all. Unlike MPs, the Lords did not feel any pressure from voters, so that is <u>exactly</u> what happened.

The government even seemed to be delaying its own Bill! Perhaps they'd only introduced it to get rid of Benjamin Spoor's Bill? Hmmm.

There was a lot of debate in both houses and a few amendments, including:

1) Removing the second clause; 2) Allowing a woman with a university degree to become a solicitor in three years instead of five, same as a man, 3) Allowing professional societies to admit women; and 4) Allowing universities to admit women and give them degrees.

Both houses needed to agree on ALL the changes.

The moral of this story is: If you want support for your cause, write to your MP!

Did You Know...?

Apparently, MPs received so many letters from women, asking them to support the Women's Emancipation Bill, that some of them were scared to oppose it!

Parliament (Qualification of Women) **Act** November 1918

11th November 1918
The First World War ends.

21st November 1918
Parliament (Qualification of Women) Act

And the clock was ticking as the end of the year approached! Finally, on 23rd December, the last working day of 1919, Parliament passed the Sex Disqualification (Removal) Act and King George V gave it his Royal Assent.

YIPPEE! (SORT OF)

The Sex Disqualification (Removal) Act only did about one-third of what Benjamin Spoor's Bill would have. How disappointing! But perhaps taking a small step towards a fairer world is better than taking no steps at all.

Despite the disappointment, one thing was true: this law allowed women to become barristers and solicitors – and to start making legal history! And that is exactly what they have done.

WHAT HAPPENED NEXT?

There was no time to waste! The very next day, Helena Normanton applied to train as a barrister at Middle Temple; and the first female justices of the peace were appointed. Over the next century, Parliament has continued to make laws that make life – and work – fairer for women.

Did You Know...?

A *justice of the peace* (also called a 'magistrate') is a local judge who hears less serious criminal cases, and cases that involve children and families. You don't need to be a qualified lawyer to be a justice of the peace, but you do need common sense and good judgment.
By 1948, there were over 3,000 female magistrates!

14 December 1918
Constance Markievicz is elected as an MP.

1st December 1919
Nancy Astor takes her seat in the House of Commons.

THE SEX DISQUALIFICATION (REMOVAL) ACT OF 1919

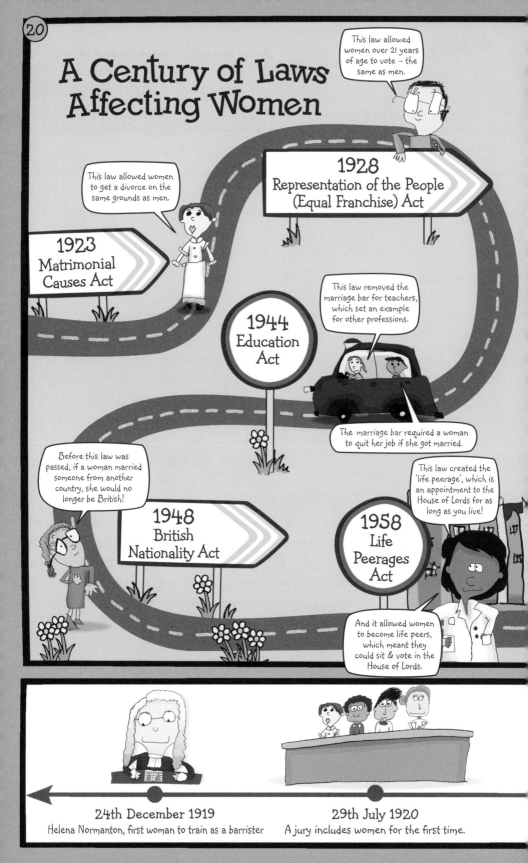

History Makers

Each History Maker has her own story, yet she shares a lot with the others – like hard work, persistence and a belief that everyone deserves a fair chance for a good life. At some point in her life, every one of these women simply decided she COULD and WOULD make a difference, and that's why she made history!

1 Barbara Leigh Smith Bodichon
8th April 1827 to 11th June 1891

Campaigner for fairer laws and supporter of university education for women

At the age of 27 and even though she had no legal education, Barbara wrote *A Brief Summary in Plain Language of the Most Important Laws Concerning Women*. This booklet was published in 1854; it explained the laws that affected women unfairly, especially when it came to property and work.

Barbara's booklet inspired people to try to reform the Law. So she put together a committee to do just that. She didn't stop there! In 1858, she and Bessie Rayner Parkes launched a magazine for women; in 1859, she & Jessie Boucherett started a society to support women's employment; and in 1869, Barbara, Lady Stanley and Emily Davies founded Girton College, the first women's college of Cambridge University.

Busy Barbara! Although she did not live long enough to see laws that allowed women to vote or become lawyers, her work was a big step on the journey towards equal rights for women and a fairer society.

10th May 1922
Ivy Williams, first woman to be called to the Bar

18th December 1922
Carrie Morrison, first female solicitor in England

② Helen Taylor
27th July 1831 to 29th January 1907

First woman to <u>try</u> to run for Parliament

Helen believed every adult should be allowed to vote and that all children should have access to free primary education. She fought for these beliefs and worked hard for her community. As a member of the London School Board, she made sure that poor children had boots and a meal at school – even if she had to pay for them herself!

In 1885, Helen was selected by the Camberwell Radical Club as their candidate for MP. Yippee! But when she presented her nomination to the Presiding Officer, he wouldn't accept it. He said the law referred to candidates as 'him' or 'he', so a woman could not be a candidate. Boo on him!

Helen may not have been allowed to become an MP, but that didn't stop her from working hard to make life better for everyone.

③ Eliza Orme
25th December 1848 to 22nd June 1937

First woman to be granted a law degree

In 1873, Eliza started working in a barrister's chambers, writing property agreements. Even though she had attended university and her work was excellent, she was NOT allowed to be a lawyer! Despite this, she set up her own practice and did agreements for others. In 1888, she was granted a well-deserved law degree from University College London.

Matrimonial Causes Act
June 1923

Representation of the People (Equal Franchise) Act
July 1928

26th June 1923
Matrimonial Causes Act

2nd July 1928
Representation of the People (Equal Franchise) Act

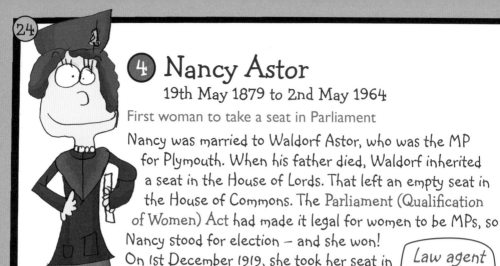

④ Nancy Astor
19th May 1879 to 2nd May 1964

First woman to take a seat in Parliament

Nancy was married to Waldorf Astor, who was the MP for Plymouth. When his father died, Waldorf inherited a seat in the House of Lords. That left an empty seat in the House of Commons. The Parliament (Qualification of Women) Act had made it legal for women to be MPs, so Nancy stood for election – and she won! On 1st December 1919, she took her seat in the House of Commons, just a few weeks before the Sex Disqualification (Removal) Act was passed.

> Law agent was what we called a solicitor in Scotland!

⑤ Madge Easton Anderson
12th August 1896 to 9th August 1982

First female law agent in Scotland

In 1916, Madge received an Arts degree from Glasgow University, her first step to becoming a law agent. Next, she appreticed for two years at a law firm, where her boss supported her. That was Step #2.

In 1917, Madge began studying Law at the University of Glasgow (Step #3). So, when the Sex Disqualification (Removal) Act was passed, Madge was all set. She applied to take the law agent exam but was rejected. The Incorporated Society of Law Agents claimed that her apprenticeship

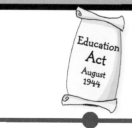

Education Act
August 1944

British Nationality Act
July 1948

19th January 1944
Education Act

30th July 1948
British Nationality Act

Did You Know...?

Nancy Astor was NOT the first woman to be <u>elected</u> as a Member of Parliament! In 1918, Constance Markievicz was the first woman to be elected as an MP, but she refused to take her seat because she did not want to swear allegiance to King George V of England.

...idn't count because it had taken place before the law was passed! So Madge ...ook her case to court – and won. She passed the exam in October 1920 and ...ulfilled her ambition. She wasn't going to let ANYTHING stop her!

6 Carrie Morrison

3rd February 1888 to 20th February 1950

First female solicitor in England & Wales

During the First World War, Carrie worked at MI5, where she met Alfred Baker. After the war, she worked at his law practice and, as soon as the Sex Disqualification (Removal) Act was passed, he offered her a training contract to become a solicitor. So, in 1922, Carrie became the first woman to become a solicitor in England & Wales!

Carrie spent her career giving legal help to poor people in London's East End. She believed in fairness – for everyone – and she devoted her life and work to acting on that belief.

1946
Women are allowed to become diplomats.

1948
Margaret Kidd, first female King's Counsel

7 Ivy Williams

7th September 1877 to 18th February 1966

First woman to be called to the Bar

> Being *called to the Bar* means you're allowed to argue a case in court!

Ivy attended university lectures at the Society of Oxford Home Students. She passed her exams in 1903, but she had to wait for the Sex Disqualification (Removal) Act to train as a barrister. Then she had to wait until 1920, when Oxford University started awarding degrees to women, to get her degree! Ivy completed training and passed her exams with flying colours. She was called to the Bar on 10th May 1922. She never practised as a barrister, but she did teach Law at the Society of Oxford Home Students. A great teacher and learner, Ivy taught herself Braille when her eyesight failed!

> The phrase comes from the Middle Ages when a wooden bar separated the judge from the people in a courtroom. The judge would only call a qualified person to the bar to argue the case.

8 Helena Normanton

14th December 1882 to 14th October 1957

First woman to train as a barrister; first woman to practise as a barrister in England and one of the first female King's Counsel

When the Sex Disqualification (Removal) Act received its Royal Assent, Helena was ready. She

1956
Rose Heilbron, first female judge

Life Peerages Act

April 1958

30th April 1958
Life Peerages Act

started training as a barrister the very next day! Helena had waited for this moment for a <u>long</u> time. She had grown up without a father and had seen her mother struggle, simply because she was a woman on her own. When she was 12, Helena went with her mother to see a solicitor; her mum didn't understand his advice, but Helena did. That moment inspired her to become a barrister.

Helena believed that women should have the same rights as men. She campaigned for equal pay for equal work. Even though, thanks to the Representation of the People Act, she herself could vote, she pushed for voting rights for ALL women. In her work, she served mostly female clients and helped other women become barristers. In 1949, she and Rose Heilbron became the first English women to be made King's Counsel.

Helena was a lifelong activist, always ready to stand for her beliefs. She even took part in a protest against the atomic bomb at the age of 70!

Did You Know...?
Helena Normanton was the first married woman to have a British passport in her maiden name!

9 Margaret Kidd
14th March 1900 to 22nd March 1989

First female barrister in Scotland and first woman to be appointed as King's Counsel

Margaret REALLY wanted to be a diplomat in the civil service. Unfortunately, while the Sex Disqualification (Removal) Act allowed women to do lots of jobs – solicitor, barrister, vet, accountant – it did NOT allow them to work overseas for the civil service! So she decided to be a barrister instead. The legal world

1965
Elizabeth Lane, first female High Court judge

Equal Pay Act May 1970

29th May 1970
Equal Pay Act

must be happy she did. In 1922, Margaret became the first woman to join the Faculty of Advocates (the Scottish Bar), and, until 1948, she was the ONLY female barrister in Scotland! Margaret made lots of history. She was the first female barrister to appear before the House of Lords, the first female judge in Scotland and the first woman to be appointed King's Counsel.

> The *Inns of Court* are professional organisations for barristers. There are four of them: Gray's Inn, Lincoln's Inn, Inner Temple and Middle Temple.

Even though she wasn't allowed to be a diplomat, Margaret committed herself to the job she WAS allowed to do. By doing that, she made history!

10 Rose Heilbron
19th August 1914 to 8th December 2005

First woman to become a judge in England; first woman to lead an English murder case and one of the first female King's Counsel

Rose studied Law at the University of Liverpool. After graduating, she received a scholarship to join Gray's Inn. She earned a Master of Laws degree, but when she applied for a pupillage, she was rejected. The reason? You guessed it – because she was a woman. So Rose

Did You Know...?
Being a King's Counsel ('KC') meant that a barrister was recognised by the King as one of "His Majesty's Counsel Learned in the Law." It's a HUGE honour that is only granted to a truly outstanding barrister. These days, the honour is called Queen's Counsel ('QC') because our current monarch is Queen Elizabeth II.

Criminal Justice Act Section 25 October 1972

26th October 1972
Criminal Justice Act

1974
Barbara Calvert, first female Head of Chambers

went back to Liverpool, completed a pupillage and started working on criminal cases. Some people thought this work was too violent for a woman, but Rose proved them wrong. By the time she was 31, she had worked on ten murder cases. In 1949, she defended George Kelly in a famous murder case (even though he'd wanted a 'fella' to be his barrister).

> A *pupillage* is a period of training that barristers do before they start to practise.

In 1949, Rose and Helena Normanton were the first English women to become King's Counsel. In 1956, she was appointed the Recorder of Burnley – the first female judge in England.

11 Elizabeth Lane
9th August 1905 to 17th June 1988

First female county court judge and the first female High Court judge in England & Wales

Elizabeth wasn't that interested in school; she liked hockey and having fun. So, even though she passed the entrance exams, she decided not to go to university. Instead she went to Canada, where she met Randall Lane. They fell in love, came back to England and got married. Randall wanted to be a barrister and Elizabeth decided to study along with him. She thought it would be a 'miracle' if she passed the exam, but indeed she DID!

Elizabeth was called to the Bar in 1940. After her pupillage, she worked for anyone who needed help, even if they were poor. Perhaps this experience developed her compassion, fairness and understanding – all of which made her a good judge! Elizabeth became a High Court judge in 1965. For the first time ever, barristers had to use the phrase 'My Lady' when speaking to a judge.

Sex Discrimination Act November 1975

12th November 1975
Sex Discrimination Act

1979
Margaret Thatcher, first female prime minister

> Barristers are self-employed, so they join a *chambers* which provides office space and staff to support their work.

12 Barbara Calvert
30th April 1926 to 22nd July 2015
First female Head of Chambers in the Temple

After Barbara studied at the London School of Economics, she worked as a mother and homemaker. Then, one night at a party, she started chatting to someone who suggested that she might enjoy working as a barrister.

She decided to give it a try; she joined the Middle Temple, took a special course and passed the exams. In 1961, at the age of 35, Barbara was called to the Bar. Initially, she worked at the chambers of John Platts-Mills; but in 1974 she set up her own chambers (4 Brick Court). Barbara fought for women, children and grandparents' rights and she treated her clients very well. She also supported other women and young people who wanted to become barristers. She became a Queen's Counsel in 1978 and she was the first woman to argue a case in the European Court of Human Rights. Barbara had a real zest for life. She often bicycled to court and, legend has it, she once rode her bicycle to a garden party at Buckingham Palace!

13 Margaret Thatcher
Baroness Thatcher
13th October 1925 to 8th April 2013
First female Prime Minister of the United Kingdom

Margaret studied chemistry at Somerville College, Oxford

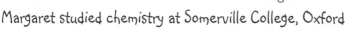

1988
Elizabeth Butler-Sloss, first female Court of Appeal Judge

1991
Association of Women Barristers is founded.

University, but always dreamed of going into politics. In 1950 and 1951, she ran for Parliament. Despite losing both times, she loved campaigning. While she waited for her chance to run again, she got married, had twins and studied Law. In 1959, she was back on the campaign trail. This time she won! She was elected as Member of Parliament for Finchley.

After completing a pupillage, a barrister usually looks for a *tenancy* in a chambers. Once you get a tenancy, you start practising as a barrister.

In 1975, Margaret challenged Edward Heath in a leadership election — and won! So when the Conservatives won a majority in the 1979 General Election, Margaret became our country's first female Prime Minister. She served until 1990 and was the longest-serving British prime minister of the 20th century.

14 Elizabeth Butler-Sloss

Baroness Butler-Sloss • Born on 10th August 1933

First female Court of Appeal judge in England and Wales

When Elizabeth was 13, she decided to become a barrister. Her brothers, who were lawyers, tried to convince her to do something else; her dad, who was a judge, told her if her brothers could do it, she could too — if

Did You Know...?

In the 1959 General Election, 81 women stood for election. 25 of them were elected! Margaret Thatcher won her seat; Elizabeth Butler-Sloss did not. The 1959 election was also Winston Churchill's final one. He was re-elected as MP for Woodford at the age of 84! As of 2019, there are 207 female Members of Parliament in the House of Commons and 206 female peers in the House of Lords.

1992
Betty Boothroyd, first female Speaker of the House

2007
Patricia Scotland, first female Attorney General

she was clever enough! Of course she WAS clever enough! Even though she didn't go to university, Elizabeth passed the exams. She was called to the Bar in 1955, at the age of 21. After a pupillage, she got a tenancy at a chambers where, in the beginning, she worked on criminal cases. Later on, she did family law cases. In 1970, she became Registrar at Somerset House — her first appointment as a judge. Nine years later, she was appointed as a High Court Judge. In 1988, Elizabeth became a Court of Appeal Judge — a 'Lord Justice of Appeal'.

A woman had never done that job, so she had to have a man's title! In 1999, she became the first female President of the Family Division. That meant she was the highest-ranking female judge in this country until 2004.

⑮ Betty Boothroyd
Baroness Boothroyd · Born on 8th October 1929
First female Speaker of the House of Commons

Betty danced with the famous 'Tiller Girl' troupe at the London Palladium. Sadly, her foot got infected and she had to give up her dream. She turned her attention to politics instead. She wanted to make sure 'normal' people had a fair chance at a good life. She ran for Parliament — not once, not twice, not three or even four times. On her FIFTH try, in 1973, Betty was elected as the Member of Parliament for West Bromwich West!

In 1992, her fellow MPs elected Betty to be the Speaker of the House of Commons. They'd never had a female speaker before, so Betty created several new customs. She decided NOT to wear the traditional Speaker's wig and announced that she should be called 'Madam Speaker'. She was Speaker until her retirement in 2000 and she now sits in the House of Lords.

Equality Act April 2010

Succession to the Crown Act April 2013

8th April 2010 Equality Act

25th April 2013 Succession to the Crown Act

Did You Know...?

The role of 'Attorney General' started back in the 13th century because the King needed a lawyer to represent him in court. The Attorney General gives legal advice to the government and government ministers; he or she also looks after ALL of the government departments that prosecute legal cases.

16 Patricia Scotland

Baroness Scotland of Asthal • Born 19th August 1955

First female Attorney General for England, Wales, and Northern Ireland; first female Secretary General of the Commonwealth of Nations

Patricia was born in Dominica, in the West Indies. Her family moved to London when she was two years old. When she was a child, she was upset by injustice; her dad asked her, "What are YOU going to do about it?"

Well, Patricia worked hard at school and studied Law. She was especially interested in constitutional, public, family and human rights law and in 1977, she was called to the Bar. In 1991, at the age of only 35, she was made Queen's Counsel – the first black woman to become a QC.

In 2007, she became the Attorney General for England, Wales and Northern Ireland – the first woman and first black person to serve in this important position. Since April 2016, she has served as the Secretary General of the Commonwealth of Nations – the first woman to hold this position. Throughout her career, Patricia has held on to her desire to fight injustice, and, as she works to make life fairer for everyone, she keeps on making history.

Yippee!
Happy reading!

2017
Brenda Hale, first female President of the Supreme Court

2019
100 Years of Women in Law!

17 Brenda Hale

Baroness Hale of Richmond • Born on 31st January 1945

First woman to be appointed to the Law Commission; first (and only) female Law Lord; first female President of the UK Supreme Court

Thanks to her lifelong love of learning and appetite for hard work, this self-described 'specky swot' has made the most of every opportunity that has come her way. The result of all her effort? She's only become the highest judge in our country!

Brenda grew up in Yorkshire. After her dad died, Brenda's mum supported Brenda and her two sisters by working as a primary school headteacher. Brenda studied law at Girton College*, Cambridge. After she graduated (first in her class, of course!) she taught Law at Manchester University; during this time, she also prepared for her law exams.

In 1969, she was called to the Bar and she worked part-time as a barrister while also teaching Law. She was very interested in laws that affected women and children. In 1984, Brenda and Susan Atkins wrote *Women and the Law*. This book showed how the Law had a biased view of life and treated women unfairly. After *Women and the Law* was published, Brenda was appointed to the Law Commission (the first woman and youngest person ever). There, she was part of a team that reviews and reforms the Law. This gave her the chance to work on better laws for women, families and children.

Do your best at whatever you're doing, and opportunities will come to you.

Brenda became a Recorder in 1989, a High Court Judge in 1994, and a Court of Appeal Judge in 1999. In 2004, Brenda became the first and only female Law Lord in the House of Lords. The Law Lords got their very own court in 2009 – the Supreme Court – and in 2017, Brenda became its first female President!

Not only does Brenda serve as our country's highest judge, she also works hard for diversity. She understands that if you're the 'first', you should hold the door open for others. That's the only way we will build a legal system that reflects our society.

*If 'Girton College' rings a bell, it's because Barbara Leigh Smith Bodichon (Page 22) helped to start it, back in 1869!

How to Make a Difference

There's no guarantee that you'll make history but you can definitely make a difference! Here's how:

STEP **1**

DECIDE that you want to make a difference!

(Deciding is the most important step!)

STEP **2**

LOOK all around you!

When you look around, you'll see lots of simple ways to make a difference — even picking up rubbish and popping it in a bin makes the world a better place!

STEP 3

QUESTION what you see!

Ask yourself WHY things are the way they are. If the answer is, "That's just the way it is," then ask again!

Remember, 100 years ago, women weren't allowed to be barristers and solicitors. That was just the way it was – until someone questioned it.

Do you recognise something that is unfair? For you? For someone else?

Do we need to change the way things are?

STEP 4

THINK about what you can do.

There are lots of small ways to make a difference every day:

Be kind.

Listen to and respect other people.

Be a good neighbour.

Recycle bottles, tins, plastic and paper.

STEP 5

DO something!

Of course, you can make a difference in big ways too:

Learn and develop new skills — so that you can use them to make a big difference!

Volunteer for a charity. Or work for a charity.

Work at a job that you enjoy and do well.

Take part in a peaceful protest.

Organise a rubbish cleanup in your neighbourhood.

Vote! If you're not old enough, remind someone else!

Contact your MP or local councillors to make your voice heard.

To find out who represents you, visit www.theyworkforyou.com.

YOUR REPRESENTATIVES:

Your Member of Parliament:

_____

Postal Address: House of Commons, Westminster, London SW1A 0AA

Your Local Councillor(s):

_____

_____

_____

The People in Our Legal System

Our legal system is the foundation that gives everyone a fair chance at a good life. There are many different jobs that people do:

People Who Make the Law

We introduce, debate and pass new laws through the Houses of Parliament!

I give Royal Assent when Parliament passes a new law!

DRAFT BILL for a fantastic new Law!

DRAFT BILL for a fantastic new Law!

House of Lords Peer

House of Commons Member of Parliament

The Queen

People Who Work in the Criminal Justice System

I look after public safety and arrest and investigate people who break the law.

I represent the accused person in a criminal trial.

I represent society in a criminal trial.

I preside at a criminal trial and look after the jury.

Police Officer   Defence Barrister   Prosecution Barrister   Criminal Court Judge

People Who Use the Law to Make Things Happen

I specialise in Family Law. I help people who want to adopt a child.

I specialise in Property Law. I help companies buy and sell buildings and land.

I specialise in Employment Law. I help companies hire people to work for them.

I specialise in Commercial Law. I help companies make agreements with each other for new products and big projects!

I specialise in Immigration Law. I help people who move to a different country.

Solicitors Who Specialise in All Sorts of Legal Areas

People Who Work in the Civil Justice System

I represent my client who has made a legal claim against someone.

I defend my client against the legal claim that someone has made.

I preside at the civil hearing and decide on the outcome of the legal claim.

Our legal system needs lots of people, who all do their jobs well. And of course, it needs you, too!

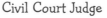

Decision

aimant Barrister   Defence Barrister   Civil Court Judge

How Parliament Makes a Law

House of Lords

1 FIRST READING
A member of the House of Lords introduces the Bill. There is no debate or discussion.

2 SECOND READING
The Lords consider and debate the Bill. If there is enough support, the House of Lords will vote.

The Bill does not pass. ◄ 'No' — The Lords VOTE on the Bill! — 'Aye' ►

3 COMMITTEE
A group of people examine the Bill word for word. They may rewrite it or make additions.

4 REPORT
The Lords discuss and debate the Bill and suggest changes. (They MIGHT vote on the Bill.)

5 THIRD READING
The Lords consider the Bill again, and they can suggest amendments.

The Bill does not pass. ◄ 'No' — The Lords VOTE on the Bill! — 'Aye' ►

Has this Bill also passed through the House of Commons?

NOT YET! Then it must also go through the House of Commons.

YES!

6 AMENDMENTS
The Lords consider changes that MPs may have made to the Bill. Both houses must agree on the EXACT words in the Bill.

ROYAL ASSENT
The Bill receives Royal Assent; it is now a Law (which is called an 'Act of Parliament').

A Bill must pass through the House of Lords **AND** the House of Commons before it can become a law.

DRAFT BILL

House of Commons

1 FIRST READING
A Member of Parliament (MP) introduces the Bill. There is no debate or discussion.

2 SECOND READING
MPs consider and debate the Bill. If there is enough support, the House of Commons will vote.

3 COMMITTEE
A group of people examine the Bill word for word. They may rewrite it or make additions.

'Aye' ← MPs VOTE on the Bill! → 'No'

The Bill does not pass.

4 CONSIDERATION
MPs discuss and debate the Bill and suggest changes. (They MIGHT vote on the Bill.)

5 THIRD READING
MPs consider the Bill again, and they can suggest amendments.

Then it must also go through the House of Lords.

NOT YET!

Has this Bill also passed through the House of Lords?

'Aye' ← MPs VOTE on the Bill! → 'No'

The Bill does not pass.

YES!

6 AMENDMENTS
MPs consider changes that the Lords may have made to the Bill. Both houses must agree on the EXACT words in the Bill.

PUZZLES

ANAGRAM ADVICE

Decipher the names, then arrange the letters in the red circles to reveal the first 3 words of Baroness Hale's advice.

1 Maize Role (HINT: First woman to be granted a law degree)

⭕ ☐ ☐ ☐ ☐   ⭕ ☐ ☐ ☐

2 Hobby Tote To Dry (HINT: First female Speaker of the House)

☐ ☐ ☐ ☐ ☐   ☐ ☐ ☐ ☐ ☐ ☐ ☐ ⭕

3 Butter Ball Shoes Size L (HINT: First female Court of Appeal judge)

☐ ☐ ☐ ☐ ☐ ☐ ☐ ☐

☐ ⭕ ☐ ☐ ☐ ☐ - ⭕ ☐ ☐ ☐ ☐

4 Mark Did Great (HINT: First female King's Counsel)

☐ ☐ ☐ ☐ ☐ ☐ ⭕ ☐ ☐ ☐ ☐

5 Canny Roast (HINT: First woman to take a seat in the House of Commons)

☐ ☐ ☐ ☐ ⭕ ☐ ☐ ☐ ☐

6 Handle Bear (HINT: First female President of the Supreme Court)

⭕ ☐ ☐ ☐ ☐ ☐ ☐ ☐ ☐ ☐

7 Hero Bores Nil (HINT: First woman to become a judge in England)

⭕ ☐ ☐ ☐ ☐ ☐ ☐ ☐ ☐ ☐ ⭕ ☐

Baroness Hale's Advice:

" ☐ ☐   ☐ ☐ ☐ ☐   ☐ ☐ ☐ ☐ ☐ "

WORD SEARCH

Search for words that are hidden forwards, backwards and diagonally.

```
h i v y w i l l i a m s o l i e r b
e v s n o t n a m r o n a n e l e h
l g b a c i l o s r t a p i l z f a
e u a n j u d g o a b r a b d a f l
m a r g a r e t k i d d r a d i c w
a l b u r b i l a e w e l r o s o g
n n a e e c a l w g n d i n b r t d
t r r e i q m r o d e d a t c o l n
o o a l z u o y a u r w m j u d g a
n t l e a e r h f j o o e n i w a l
o s e n g e a u i o n s n o z h n t
r a s a b l z g l r a g t r a a s o
b y n l e a i f z m a s b t b e c c
l c u h t r e g i w l n a a e l o s
i n o t h o e l i z a o r m e n l a
e a c e s t w o r l c u r n o t c i
h n s b y i g r e t o y i d o t y c
e o g a d c q d n e m r s y w y v i
s m n z d i u s i a m u t o e s o r
o m i i a l e t i c o j e r y e i t
r o k l m o e k i i n g r h e u n a
q u e e n s c o u n s e l t u q g p
h e l e n t a y l o r r t o n e u w
```

☑ Act
☐ Barrister
☐ Brenda Hale
☐ Commons
☐ Eliza Orme
☐ Elizabeth Lane
☐ Helen Taylor
☐ Helena Normanton
☐ Ivy Williams
☐ Judge
☐ Jury
☐ King's Counsel
☐ Law
☐ Lords
☐ Margaret Kidd
☐ Nancy Astor
☐ Parliament
☐ Patricia Scotland
☐ Queen's Counsel
☐ Rose Heilbron
☐ Solicitor
☐ Wig

PUZZLE ANSWERS

ANAGRAM ADVICE

The first three words of Baroness Hale's advice are:

"Do your best!"

Her full advice is: "Do your best at whatever you're doing, and opportunities will come to you."

1. Eliza Orme
2. Betty Boothroyd
3. Elizabeth Butler-Sloss
4. Margaret Kidd
5. Nancy Astor
6. Brenda Hale
7. Rose Heilbron

WORD SEARCH

No peeking!